NEW JERSEY
DEVILS

ALEX YANNIS

Published by Creative Education
123 South Broad Street, Mankato, Minnesota 56001
Creative Education is an imprint of The Creative Company

Designed by Rita Marshall
Cover Illustration by Rob Day

Photos by: Bettmann Archives, Bruce Bennett Studios, Focus on Sports,
Sports Photo Masters and Wide World Photos

Library of Congress Cataloging-in-Publication Data

Yannis, Alex, 1937-
New Jersey Devils / Alex Yannis.
p. cm. -- (NHL Today)
ISBN 0-88682-679-9

1. New Jersey Devils (Hockey team)--History--Juvenile literature.
[1. New Jersey Devils (Hockey team)--History. 2. Hockey--History.]
I. Title. II. Series.

GV848.N38Y36   1995   93-48436
796.962'64'0974921--dc20

123456

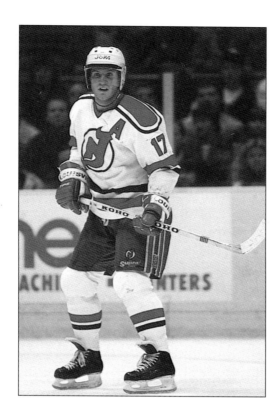

THE DEVILS COME OF AGE

The press box is the room in a sports complex where people from newspapers, radio and television report the proceedings of athletic events. But one spring night in 1988, two New Jersey Devils executives and an assistant coach turned the press box at the Chicago Stadium into a dance studio, and nobody blamed them one bit.

It was on the night of April 3, the last game of the regular season that year, that the Devils experienced the moment that stands above all others to date in the history of the franchise.

Pat Sundstrom helped the team reach the playoffs in 1988.

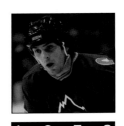

Wilf Paiement was the Colorado Rockies' leading scorer with 87 points.

On that night, John MacLean scored an overtime goal against the Chicago Blackhawks to send the Devils to their first playoff appearance. The moment MacLean's shot hit the back of the net—2 minutes and 21 seconds into the overtime, giving the Devils a 4-3 victory—the entire Devils bench spilled onto the ice in a joyous celebration that will forever be etched in the minds of the players and the fans. MacLean's goal ended six years of playing in obscurity in the New Jersey Meadowlands.

"That was definitely the most important day in the history of this franchise," said Max McNab, the executive vice president of the Devils who has been with the team since its first day in New Jersey in 1982. McNab joined Lou Lamoriello, the president and general manager, and Bobby Hoffmeyer, the assistant coach at that time, in a jubilant dance in the press box as a noisy celebration broke out on the rink below.

"There have been some other highlights," McNab recalled years later, "but that night in Chicago is the one that will go down in history as the most important step. That is the first big chapter in the history of this team."

"That was the night this franchise became of age," added Lamoriello, who joined the Devils in the 1987–88 season after two decades as the guiding force behind the successful athletic programs at Providence College in Rhode Island. "That was a big moment for this organization, a moment that people will always remember."

"You are not supposed to cheer in the press box," McNab continued, "but that was such a dramatic moment. We just couldn't help it. We were so happy, we waltzed around for a while."

"It was a moment that I don't think I will ever forget," said

In 1988, John MacLean earned the Devils a playoff spot (page 7).

Ken Daneyko, one of the cornerstones of the Devils' defense for years. "We were a group that grew up together, a group of friends. A lot of us were drafted by the Devils and we gave our heart and soul for the team, but we also played for each other."

FROM SCOUTS TO ROCKIES TO DEVILS

1 9 7 9

Menacing defenseman Barry Beck was one of Colorado's first stars.

The franchise that was to become the New Jersey Devils was born as the Kansas City Scouts when the National Hockey League held its fourth expansion draft in 1974. Unfortunately, the club experienced many financial problems, including labor strikes that delayed the construction of Kemper Arena. The Scouts were also unable to attract and sign key players. They finished at the bottom of their division two years in a row and drew equally unimpressive numbers at the box office.

By the 1976–77 season, the franchise moved to Denver, where it was renamed the Colorado Rockies (now the name of a major league baseball team). In the 1977–78 season, led by right wing Wilf Paiement's 87 points and Barry Beck's record-setting 22 goals by a rookie defenseman, the Rockies finished in second place in the Smythe Division to qualify for the playoffs. But, despite other fine players such as Paul Gardner and John Van Boxmeer, the Rockies' stay in the NHL would not last long. The team finished in last place in four of six seasons.

On June 30, 1982, the franchise was renamed the New Jersey Devils when John J. McMullen, a native of New Jersey, purchased the team from Peter Gilbert and moved the franchise to the New Jersey Meadowlands. It cost McMullen $32 million to buy and move the club. Negotiating the move of the franchise to New

Jersey was one of the most difficult business transactions in sports history because of its close proximity to two New York teams (the Rangers and the Islanders) and the Philadelphia Flyers. McMullen had to pay indemnity fees, fees for changing divisions and fees for moving. He also had to share 50 percent of the television revenues with the Rangers, Islanders and Flyers—which the Devils continue to pay to this day.

Steve Tambellini led the team in goals scored their first season in New Jersey.

"If I knew what I was getting into," McMullen said recently, "I might have never done it. It was a lot tougher than I thought. But it was all worth it because it's been exciting and it has provided a real sense of achievement. Sports is an indirect form of public service. I know this because I spent a great deal of my younger life in the government."

McMullen earned a degree in electrical engineering from the United States Naval Academy and served as a commander in the United States Navy from 1940 to 1954. He has a master's degree in naval architecture and marine engineering from the Massachusetts Institute of Technology (MIT) and a doctorate in mechanical engineering from the Swiss Federal Institute of Technology in Zurich, Switzerland. That is why everyone in the Devils camp, from Lamoriello down to the last stickboy in the locker room, refers to McMullen as "doctor."

McMullen earned his fortune from a shipping concern he established in 1957. He also owned the Houston Astros baseball team for years, but in recent years he has devoted his full attention to the Devils, of which his son, Peter, is a vice president. It was Peter's early involvement in youth hockey that captured McMullen's interest in the sport.

Scott Stevens holds the team record for assists in a season (pages 10-11).

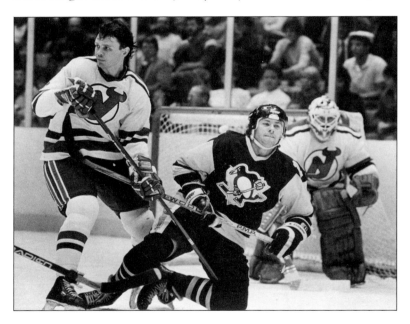

"I qualify as a 'hockey father' because Peter played in local leagues," McMullen said. "I know what the parents go through to help their children enjoy the sport. It's not easy getting up in the middle of the night driving to South Mountain."

Today, the Devils use the same South Mountain Arena in West Orange, New Jersey, as their training facility. It is a 15-minute drive from the Byrne Meadowlands Arena where the Devils play their home games. Located only eight miles from Times Square in the heart of New York City, the complex also includes Giants Stadium and the Meadowlands Racetrack.

The Byrne Arena is named after Brendan Thomas Byrne Jr., a former governor of New Jersey. He joined McMullen and John

1 9 8 3

Phil Russell joined the team as a top playmaker, adding 22 assists and 96 penalty minutes.

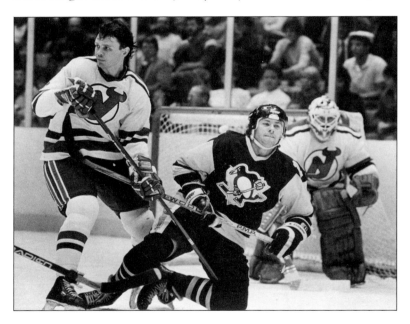

12

C. Whitehead, the Deputy Secretary of State during the Reagan presidency, as co-owner of the team. In later years, McMullen's son, Peter, and president/general manager Lamoriello were also given a small percentage of ownership of the team by McMullen.

EARLY STRUGGLES

The Devils made their debut at the Byrne Arena on October 5, 1982, a 3-3 tie with the Pittsburgh Penguins. Don Lever, the team captain, scored the first goal in Devils history, 2 minutes and 21 seconds into the game, against goalie Michel Dion.

Mel Bridgman joined the Devils at center, bringing his deft scoring touch to the team.

In their first two years in New Jersey, the Devils seemed like a direct offshoot of the New York Islanders. Billy MacMillan, who had played for the Islanders for four seasons, was the Devils' general manager and coach. Bert Marshall, who had played for six years for the Islanders, was the team's director of player personnel. Dave Cameron, Garry Howatt, Bob Lorimer, Hector Marini, Steve Tambellini and Yvon Vautour were players with an Islanders background. Another was "Chico" Resch, the popular and charismatic goaltender who had played seven seasons with the Islanders. Resch was undeniably the biggest attraction in the early days of the Devils and remains perhaps the most articulate player in the history of the team. What made Resch such an asset to the team—in addition to his capable goaltending skills—was his excellent ability to deal with the media despite long losing streaks. Resch played 106 games in his first two years with the Devils and allowed 426 goals. That's a lot of rubber, as they say in hockey.

But despite the team's early struggles, Resch maintained an upbeat attitude that spread to the rest of the team. "I must be crazy,"

13

Resch once said in the middle of a long losing streak during the Devils' first season. "I wake up each morning and I feel like the next game will start a 10-game unbeaten streak."

In reality, the longest unbeaten streak the Devils had that season was two games—both ending in ties. They ended the season with a won-lost-tied record of 14-49-13. The worst was yet to come, however.

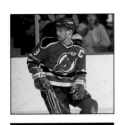

1 9 8 4

Kirk Muller was the Devils' first pick, second overall, in the Entry Draft.

SHAKING THINGS UP

In their second season, the Devils lost 18 of the first 20 games, with the 18th loss coming November 19 at the hands of the Edmonton Oilers. Wayne Gretzky, who was with the Oilers at the time, called the Devils a "Mickey Mouse" organization after the Devils' 13-4 loss to the Oilers. The comment did not sit well with the team and forced McMullen to shake up the front office and coaching staff. Tommy McVie was named head coach. McNab took over as general manager, replacing MacMillan. Marshall Johnston was hired as the new director of player personnel.

The change in personnel was the first step toward improvement for the Devils, who made Gretzky pay for his "Mickey Mouse" remark just a year later with a 5-2 triumph over the defending Stanley Cup–champion Oilers. The key play in the game came when a frustrated Gretzky threw his stick at the puck during a Devils breakaway and the Devils scored on the ensuing penalty shot.

The Devils finished next-to-last in the league that year, which gave them the second pick, behind Pittsburgh, in the draft. However, 1984 was the year Mario Lemieux, the league's most coveted player since Gretzky, was available in the draft.

The Devils were severely criticized by some for "not playing dead" in the last two weeks of the season to finish last in the

Joe Cirella scored in the 1984 All-Star Game (page 15).

Glenn Resch, New Jersey's top goaltender for the third straight season, was a favorite with fans.

league and draft Lemieux. Those who knew better, however, gave the Devils credit for their professionalism in trying to do what teams in pro sports are supposed to do: win games. General manager McNab showed the kind of integrity that earned the Devils plenty of respect throughout the sports world.

Instead of Lemieux, the Devils drafted Kirk Muller, a center who had been a member of the 1984 Canadian Olympic team. Muller scored 17 goals in his rookie year and made the NHL All-Star team that year and three more times after that for the Devils. Muller was a team leader and served as captain of the team before being traded to Montreal for Stephane Richer in 1991.

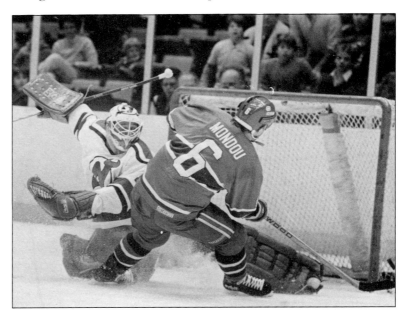

Dave Pichette was the third-highest scorer in 1985.

Aaron Broten led in both goals and assists in 1983.

Craig Billington was a tough goaltender for the Devils.

Respect for success on the ice didn't come until the spring of 1988, three months after Jim Schoenfeld replaced Doug Carpenter, who had served nearly four years as coach. Schoenfeld was hired on January 26, 1988, after the Devils fell three games below .500 (21-24-5). Schoenfeld coached the Devils to a record of 17-12-1, the culmination being the overtime victory over the Blackhawks in Chicago—the game that inspired the press box dance.

Sean Burke, the towering goaltender, was the biggest factor in the Devils' success late in the regular season that year. He joined the Devils on March 1, 1988, after concluding his stint as goaltender for the Canadian Olympic team that winter. The Devils won 10 of the 11 games he played in during the stretch run to the playoffs.

In the 1988 Stanley Cup playoffs, the Devils overcame the New York Islanders and the Washington Capitals to meet the Boston Bruins in the Wales Conference finals. Boston won Game 3 by a score of 6-1 to take the series lead. After the game, Schoenfeld, who had been a defenseman for 13 years in the NHL, accosted referee Don Koharski, saying, "Have another donut, you fat pig." The remark earned Schoenfeld a one-game suspension by the NHL. But a New Jersey court gave the Devils a temporary injunction which allowed Schoenfeld to coach Game 4. When the referee and linesmen scheduled for Game 4 learned that Schoenfeld was going to coach the game, they refused to take the ice. The start of the game was delayed until substitute officials could be found. The Devils won the game by a score of 3-1.

1 9 8 8

Before joining the Devils, Alexei Kasatonov earned his ninth Soviet League First All-Star Team honors.

Sean Burke was the first NHL rookie to start in an All-Star Game.

The NHL held a hearing on the Schoenfeld charges that resulted in Schoenfeld being suspended for Game 5. The Bruins won that game and went on to eliminate the Devils from the Stanley Cup finals in seven games.

In a season of overachievement, the Devils had come up just one game short of the Stanley Cup finals. In the next six seasons, the closest the team would come to the Stanley Cup was to lose in the opening round of the playoffs.

IN SEARCH OF GLORY

Unlike that spring of 1988, the Devils have had more talented players in recent seasons. The talent came from draft

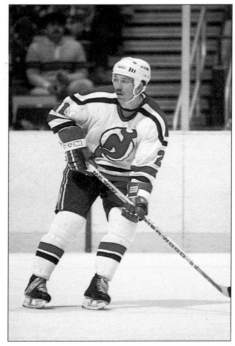

Left to right: Bruce Driver, Don Lever, Bob Lorimer, Bob Hoffmeyer.

choices, which they didn't trade away as they had in the early years, and from the addition of Russian players.

The Devils pioneered signing Russian players to the NHL. They had the foresight to draft Russian players several years ahead of everyone else in the league, with Slava Fetisov and Alexei Kasatonov among the first. In the early 1990s, the presence of Russians, Slovaks, Swedes and Finns alongside Americans and French Canadians made the Devils known as the NHL's "United Nations."

Other changes were afoot. Schoenfeld's emphasis on commitment and hard work didn't suit the personality of the team. John Cunniff, who had been an assistant coach under Schoenfeld, took over as head coach less than two months into the 1989–90 season. Cunniff, a likable and quiet man who took his frustrations out on himself rather than others, couldn't get the Devils to work up to their potential either. In the spring of 1991, with the team in danger of missing the playoffs, Tom McVie replaced Cunniff to become head coach of the team for the second time in his career.

1 9 9 3

Hall-of-Famer Jacques Lemaire was named head coach of the Devils.

McVie accomplished his mission to take the team to the playoffs. But disaster came in the first round. The Devils' opening-game victory was followed by an overtime contest in Game 2 that ended when Penguins rookie Jaromir Jagr scored and tied the series. The Devils won two of the next three games and had a chance to eliminate the Penguins on home ice. But the Penguins came on strong, winning Game 6 with a score of 4-3.

"That loss in Game 6 to Pittsburgh at home was the toughest, in my estimation," McNab recalled when asked to name the team's hardest loss. "We thought we had it after winning in Pittsburgh to go up 3-2 in games." The Devils were so devastated after los-

Claude Lemieux is one of the Devils' top scorers (pages 26-27).

1 9 9 3

Left wing Tom Chorske tallied 19 points in 50 games with New Jersey.

ing that game that they were completely out of sync in the seventh and deciding game when the series returned to Pittsburgh. The Penguins won Game 7 and went on to capture their first Stanley Cup championship.

The hiring of Herb Brooks and Robbie Ftorek during the summer of 1991 to work for the organization put McVie in a precarious position for the 1991–92 season, but McVie survived the season, which ended with a loss to the Rangers in Game 7 in the first round of the playoffs.

With Brooks sitting in the wings, the elimination by the Rangers made it easier for Lamoriello to put Brooks in McVie's place for the beginning of the 1992–93 season. Under Brooks—who had coached the United States to the gold medal in the 1980 Winter Olympics in what is remembered as the "Miracle On Ice"—the Devils justified their reputation for being one of the most difficult teams to coach.

Brooks performed no miracles for the Devils and was gone even before fulfilling the first of his three-year contract. He resigned after the Devils were eliminated by the Penguins in the first round of the playoffs, giving Lamoriello the opportunity to add yet another name to the long list of coaches in the team's short history.

The resignation of Brooks turned out to be a blessing in disguise. In the summer of 1993, the Devils hired Jacques Lemaire as their eighth coach in the history of the franchise. Lemaire, a member of the Hockey Hall of Fame, had won eight Stanley Cup championships as a player in 12 years with the Montreal Canadiens. The Devils added more winning tradition to their team by hiring Larry Robinson, the legendary Canadiens defenseman, to be Lemaire's assistant.

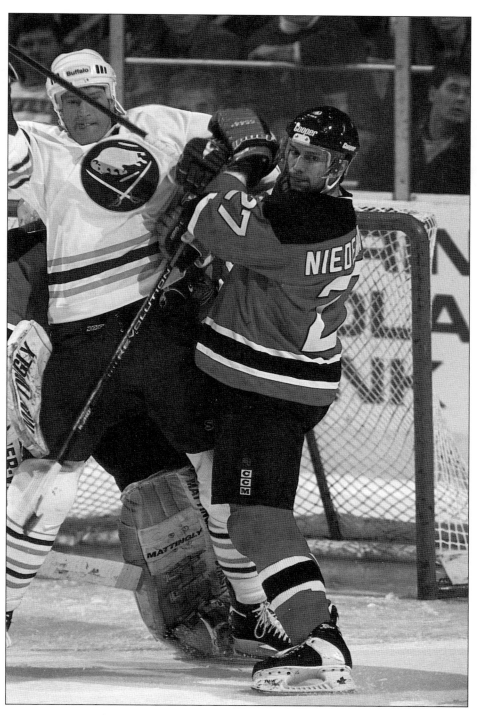

Scott Niedermayer was named to the 1993 NHL All-Rookie Team.

Lemaire and Robinson inspired the Devils and established an identity strong enough to place the team in the league's upper echelons. The Devils eliminated Buffalo and Boston in the 1994 Stanley Cup playoffs before losing to the New York Rangers (who would go on to claim the Cup) in the semifinals.

"We have some great young players in the group," McNab said. "There is something about togetherness in our sport and we have guys who are friends. They say you go to the wall for a team-mate, but you go through the wall for a friend."

And the Devils were ready to go through some walls together. They overcame the hurdle of the shortened 1995 season by putting together a game plan that emphasized teamwork. By the end of the year, the team was made up of players who had played together all season and a strategy that frustrated opponents. New

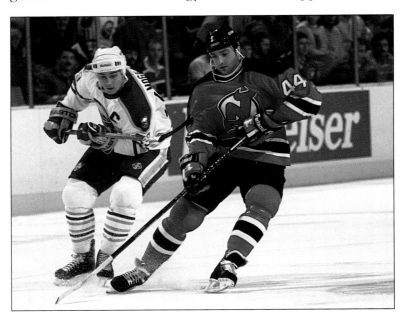

Ken Daneyko was a top performer for 11 seasons.

Jersey was also playing amid rumors that the team might be moved to Nashville. Some people didn't think there was enough room for three teams—the Devils, the New York Islanders, and the New York Rangers—in one metropolitan area. New Jersey players and fans didn't agree, and the threat of the team's move brought them even closer together. In the end, it was that sense of unity that helped them overcome every obstacle on their way to the Stanley Cup.

After finishing the regular season tied for 9th place, the Devils defeated Boston, Pittsburgh and then Philadelphia in the first three rounds of the playoffs. Coach Lemaire's strategy was to bottle up opponents in the neutral zone and take advantage of turnovers. It wasn't a flashy game plan, but it worked effectively, especially against Detroit in the finals.

New Jersey shut down the Red Wings' offensive game completely, limiting the highest-scoring Western conference team to only seven goals in the series. New Jersey won the first two games on the road and then demolished Detroit 5-2 in both Game 3 and 4 for the sweep.

As the final seconds ticked off the clock of Game 4, Mike Peluso mirrored the sentiment of the whole team as tears poured down his face. In twelve years, New Jersey had gone from a "Mickey Mouse" team to No. 1 in the NHL. It was a journey that took all the heart and guts the team could muster. But as they skated around Meadowlands Arena on June 24, 1995, holding the Stanley Cup high above their heads, they knew it was worth it.